MY GUARDIAN ANGEL PRAYER BOOK

Written by Bart Tesoriero
Illustrations by Emiguel Bojie Puod

TABLE OF CONTENTS

Library of Congress Control Number: 2011910738
ISBN 978-1-936020-25-6

Who Are the Angels?

Angels are God's invisible messengers. They are pure and holy. Angels see God face-to-face. They worship and praise Him at all times. The Bible teaches that God sends angels from heaven to earth to help us and to bring us His messages. God has His angels watching over us always.

In the Bible angels appear in different ways. Sometimes they appear in bright glory, as they appeared to the shepherds in Bethlehem on the night that Jesus was born. Sometimes angels appear to people while they sleep. An angel appeared to Joseph in his dreams to tell him that Mary was pregnant with Jesus. Sometimes angels appear as humans. Abraham met three strangers, whom he invited into his tent for a meal. Later, Abraham realized that they were truly angels.

Angels also protect us. A long time ago an angel protected the prophet Daniel when he was thrown into the lions' den. The Archangel Raphael protected Tobiah and his wife Sarah from the devil. An angel freed Saint Peter from prison by breaking his prison chains and leading him safely out to freedom—even though Peter was tied up between two soldiers!

The Bible tells us that angels worship only God. The Church, the people of God, joins with the angels in adoring God. The angels are happy when we come to know and love God, because God is wonderful!

Our Guardian Angels

Each one of us has a Guardian Angel to watch over us and protect us. At the moment we are born, each of us is given a Guardian Angel to go along with us through our life. Our angel has a name and is always with us. Our angel loves us very much and follows us wherever we go. Our Guardian Angel helps us to follow Jesus.

Jesus once said: "Make sure you do not harm any one of My little children. I tell you that their angels in heaven always look upon the face of My heavenly Father."

After Jesus went back into heaven, an evil king named Herod threw Saint Peter into prison. All of the disciples and friends of Jesus prayed for Peter. God heard their prayers, and He sent a strong and powerful angel to the prison. The angel removed Peter's chains. Peter thought he was dreaming. However, when the angel led Peter past the guards, outside the prison, and into freedom, Peter realized that God had sent an angel to deliver him.

Our Guardian Angels are always there to help us. They are our partners on the path to heaven. Let us call on our Guardian Angels to protect us and to help us always follow Jesus!

Saint Michael the Archangel

Saint Michael the archangel is God's most trusted angel, and he carries out heaven's commands. Saint Michael is a fierce warrior, protector, and comforting guardian. Saint Michael is heaven's most powerful archangel.

In the Old Testament, the prophet Daniel calls Michael "one of the chief princes" and the guardian of God's people, Israel. The very name, *Michael*, means "who is like God." This is a good name for an angel who acts with great authority, as a helper to God. Saint Michael is a champion of goodness and justice.

A long time ago an angel named Lucifer was very proud. He wanted to sit on the throne of heaven. He convinced many of his fellow angels to disobey God and turn away from Him. That is how Lucifer became the devil.

A great war broke out in heaven. Saint Michael the Archangel and the good angels fought Lucifer and the bad angels. They defeated the bad angels and threw them out of heaven. That is why Saint Michael is shown wearing armor and fighting the devil. Let us ask Saint Michael to fight the devil for us. He will help us.

Saint Michael also helps those who are sick and those who are dying. Let us pray the Saint Michael Prayer every day!

Saint Gabriel the Archangel

The archangel Gabriel is one of God's most special angels. Gabriel was the angel who appeared to the Virgin Mary. He told her the good news that God had chosen her to be the mother of His Son, Jesus.

Saint Gabriel the Archangel was always a messenger of important news. In the Old Testament, Gabriel appeared as a man to the prophet Daniel. He helped Daniel to understand a vision. Saint Gabriel also told Daniel that God would send a Savior and Messiah to Israel.

In the New Testament, the Virgin Mary had a cousin named Elizabeth. She and her husband Zechariah were very old and did not have any children. The archangel Gabriel appeared one day to Zechariah. He said, "I am Gabriel, and I stand before God." The angel told Zechariah that Elizabeth would bear him a son. They were to name him John. He would grow up to be a great prophet—Saint John the Baptist. Zechariah did not believe Gabriel's message. Therefore, Gabriel made Zechariah unable to talk, until his son John was born.

A few months later God sent Gabriel to announce to the Virgin Mary that God had chosen her to be the mother of the Messiah. Mary said, "Behold, I am the handmaid of the Lord. May it be done to me according to your word." Then the angel Gabriel left her, and returned to heaven.

Saint Raphael the Archangel

The name Raphael means *God heals*. In a wonderful story Saint Raphael the Archangel helps a boy named Tobiah to cure his father's blindness.

In the Bible, the book of Tobit tells the story about Raphael and a man named Tobit, who lived long before Jesus was born. Tobit was a good man who helped the poor. One night he suddenly lost his sight. He became blind. He could not see anything. This made him very sad. Tobit prayed very hard. He asked God to heal him. God heard the prayers of Tobit, and He sent Raphael to help him.

Tobit sent his son, Tobiah, on a journey. Tobiah went to visit his relatives who lived in a far distant land. Saint Raphael appeared as a man to Tobiah. Raphael told Tobiah that he was related to him, and he went with him on the journey. A few days later, Tobiah caught a fish. Raphael told him to take out the fish's stomach and inner parts. He said these parts of the fish could help cure Tobiah's father, Tobit.

Some time later, the two travelers returned home. Saint Raphael told Tobiah to rub the fish on his father's eyes. When he did, Tobit could see again! Then Raphael said, "I am Raphael, one of the seven angels who enter and serve before the Glory of the Lord." He told Tobit and Tobiah to praise and thank God. Then he returned to heaven.

Guardian Angel Prayers

Daily Prayer to My Guardian Angel

O Angel of God, my Guardian dear,
to whom God's love commits me here.
Ever this day be at my side,
to light and guard, to rule and guide. Amen.

A Child's Guardian Angel Prayer

Guardian Angel from heaven so bright,
Watching beside me to lead me aright,
Fold thy wings round me, and guard me with love,
Softly sing songs to me of heaven above. Amen.

Prayer to My Guardian Angel

Dear Guardian Angel, I am glad that God gave you to me!
Thank you for protecting me and being with me always.
Help me feel God's love when I am sad, and help me to
become more like Jesus, who loves me forever! Amen.

Bedtime Angel Prayers

Angel Blessing at Bedtime

Angels bless and angels keep;
Angels guard me while I sleep.

Bless my heart and bless my home;
Bless my spirit as I roam.

Guide and guard me through the night;
and wake me with the morning's light. Amen.

Prayer to My Angel Before I Go to Sleep

Dear Angel, please keep me till morning;
Please guide me all through the night.
Please comfort me when I am sad,
And help me to win the fight.

Dear Angel, please watch over my soul,
And show me better ways.
Please guard me while I am sleeping,
And keep me in all my days.

Good night my dear Angel! Amen.

Morning Prayer to My Guardian Angel

Good morning my dear Guardian Angel! God sent you from heaven to care for me, because He loves me. He gave you to guide me, to protect me, and to give me His light. He sent you to be my friend and my helper. You will show me the right way back if I should ever stray from Him.

Shelter me under your wings. Direct my steps this day. Give me confidence when I am sad, and teach me when I make mistakes. Please stay very near to me, and keep me safe from any wicked or bad spirits.

Help me find a quiet place today to think of Jesus. Help me to feel Jesus' love for me in my heart. Remind me that God thinks about me always, and that my heart is good. Help me to obey my parents and to love others.

I love you, my dear Guardian Angel! I hope to see you someday, when you bring me safely home to heaven, with my Mommy and Daddy and all my loved ones. I want to go to heaven someday, to live forever with God my Father, with Jesus, and with His precious Holy Spirit. There we will be joyful with Mother Mary, dear Saint Joseph, and all the angels and saints, safe and sound forever. Amen.

Holy Guardian Angels

Feast Day: October 2

Dear Angel at my side, my good and loyal friend, you have been with me since the moment I was born. You are my own personal guardian. God gave you to me to be my guide and protector, and you will stay with me till I die.

You helped out in great joy at my Baptism, when I became part of Jesus in a special way, by becoming a member of His Body, which is the Church. On that day I became a child of God and Jesus came into my heart.

Dear Angel, you see the dangers that are in my path, and you help me to avoid them. You help prepare my soul to receive Jesus in Holy Communion. Even though you adore Him always, you are not able to receive Him as I can.

Help me, my dear Angel, to appreciate these gifts! Help me to realize, as you do, that to serve Christ is to be a king! Help me always to avoid evil, to do good, and to keep my soul from sin. Protect me also from all danger in my life each day.

I know that someday each person on the earth will die. When that time comes, help me to be brave and to trust in God. I ask you to please go with me to meet God at the end of my life, so that we can live together with Him forever in heaven. Amen.

Prayer to Saint Michael the Archangel

Saint Michael the Archangel, defend us in battle. Be our protection against the wickedness and snares of the devil. May God rebuke him, we humbly pray; and do thou, O Prince of the heavenly host, by the power of God, cast into hell Satan and all the evil spirits, who wander through the world seeking the ruin of souls. Amen.

Prayer to Saint Michael for the Church

O glorious Saint Michael, you are the guardian and defender of the Church of Jesus Christ. Please come to the aid of our Church, as we bring Jesus to our world. It is true that the devil may try to stop the Church, but he cannot succeed. Our Lord Jesus has already won the battle against him. Please help our Holy Father the Pope and all the people of God to keep loving Jesus and to keep bringing His Word and Sacraments to the world.

O dear Saint Michael the Archangel, watch over us during life, and defend us from the attacks of the devil and his bad angels. Help us especially at the hour of our death. Please help us be ready to meet God. Obtain for us the happiness of beholding Him face to face forever. Amen.

Spiritual Armor Prayer

Heavenly Father, thank You that I am Your beloved child. You want me to be strong in You.

Today I ask you to please give us Your truth as a belt tight around our minds.

Help us to announce Your good news of peace to others as shoes for our feet.

We put on Your goodness, O Jesus, as our armor, for You have saved us and You live in our hearts.

We put on our hope to be saved as a helmet for our head.

Father, we take up faith as a shield, which is able to put out all the fiery darts of the devil.

We also take up the sword of the Spirit, which is Your Word, O Lord.

Send us dear Saint Michael and all the heavenly angels to help us win the fight for You, dear Jesus. All for You! Amen.

Prayer to Saint Raphael the Archangel

O God, in Your generous goodness, You have sent Your blessed Archangel Saint Raphael to help us when we travel. We ask You to please send him now to help us. May he lead us both on our earthly journeys and in the way of salvation. May he help us in all our trials and tests.

Dear Heavenly Father, thank You that You work all things together for the good for those who love You. May Saint Raphael, the great archangel who stands forever in worship at Your throne, present our prayers to You. We pray this in the name of Jesus. Amen.

Prayer Before Starting on a Journey

My holy Angel Guardian Saint Raphael, please ask the Lord to bless the journey which I undertake. May I have a good time and a safe time. Help me also to be good to everyone I meet, so that Jesus can shine His light through me. Help me to return safe and sound, to find my family in good health. Dear Saint Raphael, we ask you to please guard, guide, and preserve us. Amen.

Daily Prayers

The Sign of the Cross

In the name of the Father
and of the Son, ✠
and of the Holy Spirit. Amen.

The Our Father

Our Father, who art in heaven,
hallowed be Thy name.
Thy kingdom come,
Thy will be done,
on earth as it is in heaven.

Give us this day
our daily bread;
and forgive us our trespasses,
as we forgive those
who trespass against us,
and lead us not into temptation,
but deliver us from evil. Amen.

Daily Prayers

The Hail Mary

Hail Mary, full of grace, the Lord is with thee.
Blessed art thou among women,
and blessed is the fruit of thy womb, Jesus.
Holy Mary, Mother of God,
pray for us sinners,
now and at the hour of our death. Amen.

The Glory Be

Glory be to the Father,
and to the Son,
and to the Holy Spirit,
as it was in the beginning,
is now, and ever shall be,
world without end. Amen.

Daily Consecration to Mary

O Mary, my Queen and my Mother, I give myself entirely
to You. I consecrate to you today my eyes, my ears, my
mouth, my heart, my whole self without reserve. O good
Mother, as I am your own, keep me and guard me as your
property and possession. Amen.

Daily Prayers

Children's Daily Offering Prayer

By permission of the Apostleship of Prayer

Heavenly Father, I offer You this day,
All that I do, and think, and say.
Uniting it with what was done,
By Jesus Christ, Your only Son. Amen.

Act of Contrition

O my God, I am heartily sorry for having offended You,
and I detest all my sins because of Your just punishments,
but most of all because they offend You, my God, Who are
all good and deserving of all my love. I firmly resolve, with
the help of Your grace, to sin no more, and to avoid the
near occasions of sin. Amen.

Grace Before Meals

Bless us, O Lord, and these Thy gifts,
which we are about to receive from Thy bounty,
through Christ our Lord. Amen.

My Prayer to Mother Mary, Queen of Angels

Dear Mother Mary, you are my Mother in heaven. You are also the Queen of all the angels and saints. Everyone in heaven loves you, dear Mother, because you are so good and true and beautiful. I am so happy that Jesus gave you to me!

Please be with me today, dear Mother. Send the holy angels to fill me with your joy of knowing Jesus. Send them to protect me and to keep me holy. May Jesus live big in me today!

Dear Mother, I love you! Please pray for my family and friends, and for everyone in the world. God loves us all, and we praise Him forever. Amen.

Dear Mother Mary, Queen of Angels, pray for us!